On Days Such as This

Gail Dendy

Published by Botsotso in 2020
59 Natal St
Bellevue East
Johannesburg 2198
Email: botsotso@artslink.co.za
www.botsotso.org.za

ISBN: 978-1-990922-48-0

Acknowledgments

Several poems in this collection (some in modified form) have been published in:
Africa Ablaze!, Carapace, Enchanting Verses (USA), *For Rhino in a Shrinking World: An International Anthology, New Coin, New Contrast, Orbis* (UK), *Plume Poetry* (USA), *LitNet, Salzburg Poetry Review* (Austria), *the Sol Plaatje/European Union Poetry Anthology 2013, 2014 and 2017, SLIP website, Stand Magazine* (UK), *Stanzas, For want of a better word: poems from the Poetry Space Competition 2014 and Taking Note: Poems from Poetry Space Competition 2015.*

Image of a Lur, Late Bronze Age; in the National Museum, Copenhagen
Credit: The National Museum of Denmark, Department of Ethnography

Cover image: Simon Sephton

Layout and design: Vivienne Preston

Contents

III

I

Birth as a Car Crash

The damp on the side windows blocks the view.
The car won't start. I'm stranded, lost.

The mechanic's hardly more than a boy.
He leans with one hand on the door handle,
the other, imprinting itself on the roof, reminds me

if you feel something catch, change down.
He slaps the roof twice and steps back,
gives me permission to leave.

The road is a dying meteor behind me.
In my rear-view I see my life approaching

at high speed. Crashes. Stops. I step out of the car.
I am decades younger, howling, slippery with blood.
I have just begun my future.

Whisker

A single whisker –
a trembling white line
left on the carpet.
My daughter, three years old,
rubs it between thumb and forefinger
and holds it up
                to the light.

She can handle what I cannot:
its tensile beauty,
its tapering fishing-rod form,
its pale-to-darkening root,
the itch or twitch
that lets it go.

        For the cat, it's a small lost part
of the means of divination
of space and breadth.

        For my daughter, it's something
to put in her special paint box,
or to forget about.

        For me, it's the humming, buzzing
antenna we all must discover
sooner or later, persistent as
            the burnt-out wisp

of a firecracker on New Year's Eve:
a moment irrevocably gone,
        marking whatever arrives.

Billboard: Large Exclamation Mark

It was a vertical slash like that made by a madman,
or a ripper, perhaps. Or that of an artist with a house paint brush.
Or a forgotten sheet in a photographer's old lab
hung up in darkness, sans the dust. And there, beneath,

is a cosmic hole the size of a child's head.
It begins nowhere but in itself. It does not end,
cannot be taken by the hand and led.
Trust stops here, it's said.

The two companions are breached by shores
of pasty white. They swim and call, hope
for a tide to take them past the the rocks, and out. You can
drive right past: the slash, the dot. The unwritten sentence
sentences you to question every why, or what.

The Book

It was the last thing I noted
before Derek responded *Hey, lez go
down to the lake for a jol.*

He wrapped the book of me
in waterproof skins, rubbed it
till it shone like hubcaps,
popped the whole poem of me
into his canvas rucksack.

It smelled of burnt coffee
and diesel, but I made my peace
with it, and the day was half-

good, I'd say. That night I slept
rough between the paraffin stove
and the empty skottel.

Derek must've forgotten
I was there, for in the morning
he buggered off
and I spent three summers

lying on my back,
a sedentary *jolling* between seasons,
between selves, between
the long and the short of it.

But that was something
that never got noted down,
although it's stayed with me
ever since.

How to get rid of it,
I couldn't say. At any rate,
not until Derek comes back,
his hands sprouting prose,
his breath like stitches along my spine.

Selfie

In the selfie I took
with my tablet
(in technicolour, fully HD)

I saw what it is
to be old. Lines that aren't
there were suddenly
exposed. My skin, once tanned,
was the colour of stone,
and from my stone eyes,

in their blank hunks of light,
was reflected nothing,
the way dead people reflect

and living people like
to forget they could
indeed be old. The selfie

slides back into its tile
of glass. It remains
in perpetual sleep.

I shall not wake it
with the touch of a finger,
or even a kiss. I must let it keep.

Tansu[1]

Trussed in lacquer, its sheen ripening
year on year, the tansu holds out.
It was your grandmother's and, she said,

her father's before her. Someone at some time
had replaced the handles
with brass fake-18th Century ones.

They worked just as well,
two to a drawer. In winter, they were chill
as spite. One of the drawers

would never open unless you aimed straight,
had a good eye, and kicked
its corner. Then everything came

tumbling out, the craftsman's wife, barefoot,
her ivory comb still in her hand, the medicine
for the many weeks her son's illness took to cure,

a broken parasol, and those leather straps
that secured the tansu on its journey west.
The boat loaded, too, with cherry jams,

wooden coffins, chests of silk, and jade and agate
marbles which, with careless handling, had dashed
one against the other, and now were cracked.

---

[1] A Japanese chest of drawers

In My Room

The pieces of furniture
have ceased speaking.

It wasn't all that long ago
they chattered
morning and night. In the afternoons
they told secrets. Sometimes
they whispered in the language of bedding;
took umbrage at polish.

On Sundays, their sheen
was wafer thin,
their smooth exteriors dispensing
blood thoughts;
wives' tales. They housed

the cuneiform of chisels
in their deep, wooden sockets.
In their old age, they clicked
merrily as maracas
when the weather turned sour.

Now they have stopped,
are transformed
into a nest of tables,
several chairs (mismatched),
a sideboard, and a chest
of thumping drawers.

I know they're testing me. Waiting
for the moment
when I put a foot wrong,
for me to step outside the room,
give them the chance
to say what they're made of.

The Glass Girl

Had I known that your bones
were made of glass, it would have been

possible to have lifted you
with a single hand and held you up

to the light. If I had known
that your glass limbs were blown

by a renowned craftsman, I would have
created a special place to put you in.

Had I known how silent you can be,
I would have moistened my index finger

and rubbed it round and round the rim
of your limbs. Only then would you

have told me your real name, which
of course I would have fully mistaken.

The Deserted Beach

I fitted my feet into footprints
hopelessly too small,
walked half-a-dozen paces
with these odd, truncated steps
then turned around once more
to find I'd aged before my time.

What to do? Walking backwards
was no solution. Waiting
for the rising tide to lift each footprint
off its sandy base would be
merely giving in. I turned, and left.

Next day, and the next day after that,
the miniature footprints
were back, criss-crossing the beach
then looping round in spirals
before ducking up the slope
across the kikuyu grass and beyond.

But by now I had the knack,
fitting my feet into each little cup-cake print
and shortening my stride
so that these little feet
now suit me admirably
and fairly march me to our door
of thirty years before

where I hear my father saying
(that day he left for good)
not to worry, I'll be back by winter,
and then I should wear my prettiest dress,
the one that looks like wind in the blown kikuyu grass
that time the gate was left unlocked
and swung wide open for the entire day.

Story of a Zimbabwean Farm

You would search for the old place
only hesitantly, driving the 4x4
onwards down the potholed road

then, with a grind of gears, idle the engine
while you looked and looked

past the newly installed electric gates, down the tracks,
past the side of the tractor shed (now enlarged,
but the roof in need of repair),

and, finally, if you craned your neck enough,
through the soft coldness of the stone veranda.
I always wondered why you never stopped
dead, removed the keys from the ignition

and walked those last fifty paces. The new owners
would surely have let you in, shown you around.
You weren't a threat any more.

All I know is that for forty years you've stood
in your bedroom, twelve years old, your mother leaning
to kiss your feverish face, your father not yet back

from the Bush War. Wherever the vultures had circled
that day, no one would tell.
You'd had a premonition, but nothing more.

Yesterday, with the help of a tracker, (unemployed,
he said, since Mugabe's second term, his village burnt),
we found the spot, or something close enough –

a cross on rusted tin. And nothing else but knobthorns,
a duiker's shattered bone, the crackling chant of bulbul.
Those last fifty paces should be the end of the story.
But there's another one, too,

the one in which you've just turned eight
and your mother, knotting her apron behind her waist,
asks for help with slaughtering chickens.

You refuse, leave the house, slam all the doors
on your way out.

Thirteen

I was thirteen, and the Beatles
had just been unbanned.[1] The airwaves
were thick with it, the new

sounds, like dead people
being brought back to life.

But Vorster[2] was there, too,
a man perfect for radio
since he never smiled.

One flick of the dial brought
an off-station static
that was like a spell.

Each day the official News was followed
by 'Commentary', as though
one box wasn't enough
for thoughts, there had to be more,

more, which the Government provided
free instead of housing.

But I was just thirteen,
and my friends
John, Paul, George and Ringo
were out there waiting.

It was a hard day's night
about to end,
like wind-up watches, roneo machines,
one-rand notes,

and hand-washed sheets
hung up like wings.

---

[1] The Beatles' records were banned by the SABC from 1966 to 1970.
[2] Prime Minister of South Africa, 1966—1978. His dour demeanour earned him the
nickname 'Jolly John'.

Aftermath

17 June 1976. (On 16 June 1976 an uprising began in Soweto and spread countrywide, profoundly changing the socio-political landscape in South Africa. Events that triggered the uprising can be traced back to policies of the Apartheid government that resulted in the introduction of the Bantu Education Act in 1953.)

Winter tonsured a crewcut on the grass
and yet we were surprised at how the public park
bloomed as though it had relocated

from another place and settled here
in a strange and foreign land, bearing crane flowers,
agapanthus, wild irises and rows of clivia
rooted in the deep, dark earth.

I think of 'stone', 'gun' and, oddly, 'catapult'.
Or do I mean the soft furriness of caterpillar,
its pliable segments, the overabundance of legs?

In the distance, it seems the dogs have become
complacent for they leave off
their sniffing and pawing the way

wind chimes fall silent in the dead
of night. I had chimes like that, salvaged
from a dustbin, made of glass and wobbly tin,
which my mother hung on the stoep's low beam.

And how she unlatched the window that night
to calm me down and show me the partial moon, perfect
in its incompleteness, and said

believe in this, for it will come back again.
I did not know then how caterpillars come back
as bright-winged creatures, but I believed
in angels, and that was sufficient for that particular time.

The Edge of the World

My son was barely old enough to know the way home,
but in the pouring rain, the umbrella covering our heads,

he recognised the bare brick wall at the corner where
five roads meet. The wall hadn't been meant to stay like that:

the chickenwire netting, the nail gun, nails and plaster
had been ordered before I had any knowledge of the ICU's routine,

and Jack the paint man was ready with his buckets and rollers
and bag of overalls, plus assorted rags and turpentine.

After the burial and a month away, we returned to find
the wall exactly as it was before, and Jack nowhere

to be found. The five roads still met daily as if in conspiracy
(the hospital bills, for one thing, and the grief that navigates the absent

intimacy) and it seemed my son could, almost by the smell of it,
find his way up the slope of the rise which tugged him onward

as though in harness *(and wasn't that a harness you had too? immobilised*
they said, critical, and of course I kept that same polystyrene cup

till it broke apart, and afterwards the nurse rubbed my wrists and temples
with lavender water) his shoes sucking at his heels as he danced ahead,

applauding the progress of the passing cars *(I'm weeping,*
and they say it's only natural) and one lone bicycle, all splashing about

in the wet, like babies. I see that the number on our wall has lost its berth,
become an outline of itself *(and am not I, the widow,*

an outline, too, of my other self, the one rinsed for weeks in tears,
harbouring this newly shrunken space?) which our young son points at

saying *there, mommy, it's there,* before grasping my fingers
with both his hands and leading me into unfamiliar territory

where, rounding the place where five roads meet,
he tows me to the farthest point where we are now

completely lost, seeing only sea and yet more sea,
and the strip of horizon that looks like the edge of the world.

Old Photographs

1

Pointed at the camera,
the outcrop of a face
distorts in its fish-eye depths.

This could have been you.
This could have been
me, twenty or thirty years ago,
held in the blink
of a flashcube.

You'd flunked maths. I'd cheated
at science. But somehow
we graduated.
Now our twins
are lying separately
in the album, still-lifes
smiling, smiling.

II

We are not villains,
just cameras.
It's not our fault
we're no good at falsifying age.
Yes, you can cover us
with fingerprints,
retract the zoom, if you like.
You won't blind us entirely.
Everything we hatch is in the dark.

Remember
we had ancestors, too.
They turned your hair green,
your face black,
your clothes red.

III

Our shutters are programmed
to let in light. Our F-stops roam
and, see, here's your sister, gone
long before you were born, your grandfather, too,
with hat and cane, who is younger, now,
than you. They smile and smile
beneath the cellophane.
Of course smiling is not breathing,
but it's the best that we can do.

IV

Nothing will change.
Paint cannot peel from the eaves.
The cemetery cannot take more people.
In the park, a dozen brides are waiting
to have their pictures taken.
The blue bulbs flash and pop.

V

Cherry-cups. Orange tart. A table full
of still lifes.
In this dog-eared photo I discover again
what it was you thought I knew:
that you'd arrived before me and set
the table for three, not two.

VI

We record things faithfully
as only we know how. Here is a gun.
There is a broom.
A saw-toothed knife.
Life is in the practicalities.
It's what is left

when life is spent, is out.
We therefore speak
of fallibility.
We are fully qualified.

VII

Today, we're showing water.
The subjects are lying
beside the river's bank.
Time will turn them sepia
as they arrive, paddling quietly
towards an age that's unremarkable.
It's the way that they survive.

VIII

In the viewfinder, you may take
any of the images you like.
You cannot close their eyelids.
You may paste them in a book.

Make a note of how long
your life's exposure took.
It is the truth,
and loves you just as well.

Fingernails

They do not grow very fast, and I do
not let them. Their edges are ragged,
unclipped, unkempt.
The cuticles, sickle moons,
are evidence they've gone through life,
have waned and waxed
in the fire of you and me, my love.
They're familiar with earth, and soil, and mud,
have kinship with water (the soapy kind).
They know the outside, and what's within.

They are there at tender moments: baking
fairy cakes, rocking a sick child,
they have their leisure time
with paint and ink. Weekends, they're buffed
and polished with 'Mayday Pink', 'Berry Wild'.
Their smart new coats are better than a dog's.
Like new-shod horses, they ride before me
in the dark to find your mouth, your hair, your skin;
like wasps they dance and sting.

And when I'm done, and you're done
too, they'll know better than I how to be at rest,
ten horses in a paddock, knowing nothing less
than how love can keep
among rock and pollen and weed and stone, for without
my realising, you've somehow nudged
the far gate closed. I cannot arrive. You cannot go.
But for now, the horses, still ungroomed, are free to roam
on woodland, scrubland, brush and fen.
They know the race. They know the course.
I do not resent them.

Heart-to-heart

Last night the boundary wall collapsed
and mud's banked up into guttural stops
against the shed. *Mud poems you say,*
indulging in a heart-to-heart, with words
that stamp and clap and carp.

We are dizzy with the day's hot doings.
Shovels, barrows and pickaxes must winnow
what's left of scabrous dirt, heave
rocks and stones across the lawn
to withstand the future rains. We leave some
mud poems where they are, clasped
to their spot like one hand on another
the way, in misfortune, we hold each other dear.

Later, the weather changes by degrees and turns
the damp into a fleece of glass.
Yet all through winter, grass remains
on the soles of boots
and will survive, no matter what,
in fickle form, hardy as leather, yellow
as the yolk of an egg.

In time, another wall is raised.
We rinse the tools when the work is done.
Like prayers, we lay them one on one as if, complete,
we're ready now to hold each other dear,
our green hearts soaked and peeled precisely so.
In years to come, we'll strip them of their skins,
bucket them at Lent, turn them
on the flames that now burn low.

Oh, heart-to-heart, may rains not cleanse
your guttural stops, the parts
that stamp and clap and carp. Cutting loose
is all that's asked. Eschew the flame.
Adore the spark.

II

I Ask

The street has begun dancing
in between the late-fallen leaves.
No, I mean it: twisting,
twirling, turning –
is this not truly like a dance?

I ask you this
in the way I ask
about marriage.
Does it not, too, twist
and shake and turn?

Is it not
the way of leaves
unclipped from their boughs
to join in the dance?
I ask you this

and hope for a reply.
Even a short reply
will be acceptable.
I ask that you say nothing
at all about dirt, or leaves.

I see what marriage
looks like, how it stands
sometimes so quietly at the end
of our street. And it is then
that I am impelled to dance.

I do not understand it, but I ask
that you record this in your notebook
and remind me of it from time to time
when the path is frozen
and holds no imprints.

This is all I ask
and I am waiting for your reply,
and I am so very happy
at even the thought
of a single word of your reply.

The Size of Dreams

It's most elusive at a particular time
of night, between the last chores
of the evening and the hour for sleep.
It is the time when the floors are sprinkled

with shadows in black and white
the way age settles into one's hair.
This is the time when bravery opens her arms
and lets you in. You are only human, after all.

You have entered a place of water dripping
on stone. The sound of a rake working
yesterday's gravel. You wish for the world
to slow down so that you can get off

and greet the strangers in the street and ask them
your questions. You long to snap open
their hearts and touch their secretive muscles.
You hope they'll grow bigger: your longings,

your questions. You hope to survive from day to day
in a furnished room. You want to dissect whatever
leads you to bravery, perhaps in the smallest of dreams.
And then you want bigger dreams than that.

A Time for Waking

Let your heart out of its cage.
It is a bird that does not yet
know how to fly. It is
a bird that cannot yet feed itself

but knows only that there is
a time for waking and a time
for being. Wake up your heart

on a morning that is brighter
than usual, one which is clear
of sorrow, which has been swept hollow
by storm winds, making way

for new weather, new seasons.
Let your heart out of its cage
and throw away that cage:

its hinges and springs and bars,
and the tiny wooden platform
which vibrates with every beat
of your undying pulse.

Throw the cage into the night,
as far as you can. Let your heart
run undressed among the stars.

Let it breathe.
Allow it its unconfinement.
Let it answer you.

String

There's a knot around my heart
that's tightening.
Time to loosen it and find its length,
then coil it three times round
and place it in a tin.
Or wind it about the finger
as a tutorial in memory, something fixed.

It's a cat-gut thing, this string.
The stuff they used for racquets
when I was young. Tennis was simple, then.
You gave back what you got
and, with some skill, a whole lot more
if your aim was right. Nothing to get uptight
about. It was just a game.

Still, the sun bred stamina in us, enough, we said,
for forty years. Each and every day was summer.
Other seasons stalled in flight,
though once marked out with timetables and trains,
with jobs, with marriage, with whisks
and brooms and countless startled rooms.
Those days are done

and now the shadows come, leaking
across the walls and engulfing half the lawn.
In this tidal pool of umbra I fear I've drowned.
But I will not give up
my china plates, the umbrella stand that was
my gran's. Here, everything is turning dark.
I pull the string. I see the light.

Where You Are

Thunder measures out the distance
between lightning flash, and you and me.
We are still together, though separately,
two birds on up-draughts, treading air.

It wouldn't be fair to ask
where are you now? You are here
and everywhere where I can lie

and hear the roll of thunder, watch
the lightning tilting at the dark, understand
that whatever draws me back to you
is the secret within the art.

Room for Us Both

My bedroom exists in another language,
the one that has no meaning
other than itself. I cannot work it out.
I cannot find a translator for it.
All I can tell you is that it is blue
the way hibiscus blooms would be painted

blue were they not pink and red and yellow.
It is the blueness you never really see
in shadows (except in Impressionist paintings).
I cannot say it is aquamarine or
ultraviolet for then I'd be lying, and
the word *lie* is translatable and hence

exists. It is a transcendental word, perhaps
like glass. It is almost as small a word
as *skin* or *hand*. But this language
I am talking of is large and clumsy.
No, I must correct myself: it is a particular
particle, like a dust moat, only lighter.

No, I must correct myself. It is like
a stone tower that was dismantled and submerged
many centuries ago. This language has
cantilevers and barnacles. There are brown fish
and red crabs. There is khaki kelp and a single point
of reference foundering as it exhales

then inhales in sequential moments of time.
There will be a time when language arrives.
No, I must correct myself. There will be a place
where words disintegrate like a shoal of fish when you
drop your feet into water. Your feet are beautiful.
My bedroom dissolves in your mouth as I wake.

Something Missing

The house is too full of things
to be empty, yet this emptiness remains
in everything that's here: an indentation

on the carpet, the stripped wires of a cord,
a metal pot without a lid. You might say
these things have something missing,

but they're the notations bearing witness
to a life or lives well led.
And there's the rub:

One life or two? Is my present life
the spare, or heir? In which country
does my house belong? How many

things have come and gone, been
moved from room to room? I cannot
tell how full or empty this now-broken

shelf has been. I'll wait and see.
Till then, I'll say the house is full of things
that sometimes trouble others, never me.

Small Miracle

The reading-lamp like a little star
above my head. Next to me,
the cat with his moon-sized paws
and grumbling purr.
A quarter to eight: is it night
or morning? The traffic has stilled
to a heartbeat which might be my own.
Nothing about this makes sense –
an hour ago the plane I was on
sank from the sky. A river of lights
greeted the shuttle as it turned
from the airport, bearing myself and my luggage.
I felt I was part of something to be delivered.

I opened my front door to three-day old
newspapers and a wilting fern. The quiet
had hung up its clothes in my closet.
It had prepared a meal which had already
been eaten. It ushered me into my room
and undressed me. I gazed at myself in the mirror.
The child that I was gazed back.

In her hand she held a frayed rope
with wooden handles. I imagined the sounds
of her feet and the rope whipping the floor
as she skipped. This brought me back
to my senses, the flight forgotten, now,
as I unfolded my nightclothes and slipped
them on. My body felt smooth and pure.
This was not a sensation of being reborn,
but rather of dying. The glow of light was my shroud,
the room was my tomb. In the flat
next to mine, someone began practising scales
on a flute. The notes rose and fell, separate

and yet locked together. Their structure was both finite
and infinite, like a beautiful road on which
one travels at night with only the headlights
offering guidance and comfort.
In my home the succulents are beginning
to flower. I had not watered them in over a month.
This, then, is the story of a miracle. It was one
which I wrote and sent out into the world
the way a child goes out to play,
the way one discovers trust, or turns away.

Beneath the Mountain

The Elder had clothed me badly:
stockings with holes near the toes,
vests disintegrating at the armpits,
one sleeve half-hemmed. Yet I was
sufficiently dressed to go out.

The street clanged and murmured.
The lampposts counted the blessings
of wires and birds. The tarmac rose

in rapt attention beneath the many cars.
The Elder walked with me, propping me up
by the elbow, urging me
to get to wherever it was I was going.
It was not sleep I sought, but peace.

There is a mountain,
the Elder told me, *and beneath that*
place is a hill, and beneath the hill
is a mound, and so forth and so forth
until you find a grain of sand.

What should I do then? I asked.
But the Elder had already left
and I was alone in the midst

of rush-hour traffic, where coffee houses
rustled and boutiques swelled with the newest
fashions, where movie-houses flickered
like candles lit at eventide, where
the wind chimed like so many gongs.

And so I did not travel to the mountain,
but remained in the city, itself deep-hung
in a valley defined by brush and scrub.

And there was night, and there was day,
although whether the first or the last I did not know,
and one thing led to another,
and all was forgotten, or forgiven.
The Elder laid his hand upon my arm.

This is your peace, he said, and the mountain
is the shape of your longing, and the grain
of sand is the mystery into which you shall reach.

And when will that be? I queried, for I had
already grown cold, and a gust of wind
riffled the outskirts of the town. *When you*
truly know how to keep it, he replied. Or perhaps
that was merely an echo of myself that I heard.

Lightning Strike

And when a fist of lightning split
the tall pine in the corner of my garden

there was no explosion. Only pieces of flesh – no – bark,
but flesh-coloured and flushed with deadened fire, and which

became ground-borne among a flotilla of needles
and knotty twigs. I heard nothing, you understand,

but thought of Jane and Mr Rochester and how
their wondrous vows had likewise split apart in fire,

and disability, and a soul near death. The next
day it was as though the tree had awoken

once more, but not from sleep, only from pain.
And the birds took their morning feed, and drank

as though there had been no storm the previous night,
only something that had kept them awake much as

the summer solstice would. But of course this
was a winter's tale, the sun bleached to the colour of salt,

the house turning to face the half-tree's unstrapped spine
while Rochester and Jane are finally reunited. But not you

and me. We have retreated for shelter, but lacking compass and map,
we see each other only in that flash of lightning which either spills, or kills.

The Departed

When night pours into the house
I must open the windows

the way they say you must open
the windows when somebody dies.

You must open the windows
when somebody dies so as to let out

the soul. It must not become
trapped. And you must cover the mirrors

so that you may not see the face
of the mourner. Or you may see,

swiftly and manifestly, the soul
of the departed, owning the shimmering life

of it all: the linen, neatly stacked
in cupboards, the teacups on the draining board,

the last dregs of milk turning sour.
Also, the soft roundness of the cakes

that the comforters bring and have left
for you, Widow. And so I must open the windows

and the dark pours in like molasses
and it is rich, and wholesome,

and hurries on to where it must be, to where
I am now, safe and snug in the thick of things.

On Days Such as This

Miraculously, my fingernails were growing again, not very long, but no longer
the ragged strips they had been before. I was a woman once more,

but then, I felt, I might be the only one left on earth. The only single one, that is.
Everywhere I looked, there were couples. The parks, the malls, the restaurants. No one,

it seemed, was all alone. But I had embarked upon my Grief and seemed to be
no more than a prop left over from a play.

I realised the play was one in which I'd been the central character. But the text and all
its lines had been hidden from my sight. Indeed, the entire plot had been withheld from me
until the very last moment.

We made good companions for a while, she and me, I must admit. Grief did her best
to clean the house and feed the cats. She watered and pruned the garden. She went
daily to work.

I began to wonder if Grief was not real at all, but some sort of angel. She was ugly,
though, and her moods reared up like horses breaking through the yard at night.

In the morning I might see hoof prints on the walls and ceilings. Sometimes
the prints were cleft, which seemed unusual. Here and there I found hairs, hard as bristles,

left on chairs, the mat, my desk, the countertops. Now and again, the back yard smelled
of dung. I asked, in no uncertain terms, for Grief to leave. I did not, you understand,

want my old life back, only to be realigned with my former self. I wanted peace, and solitude.
But it seemed I had grown smaller, like a child's shadow upon a beach.

I knew that horses were stabled there nearby. They formed a congregation.
They, too, I discovered – but only much, much later – were part of the play
of which I had no text.

I consulted with my friends. Their advice was simple. *Open up your thoughts,* they said.
And this is what I did, having been silent for far too long,

and unhappy, too. For without a voice I had become less than myself, and more
than once had felt that, should I disappear, there would remain an echo

that followed everywhere I went, and that its ceaseless chatter would be the death of me,
yet this would bring me back to life once more. But a different life, one which would not be

mine, but in some way possessed by me so that I would no longer be alone,
or perhaps not entirely. And now the horses stand so very quietly, nudging

at the long grass that gathers up their limbs, their paddock rustling with birds and clothed in
brightest green. And this is the colour I run through on days such as this.

III

III

From Out of Left Field

The hedge is more verdant this summer. Its green reef surges
as I drop beneath its shallows. Everything seems seaborne, including

mice, pinned beneath the dwarf bamboo. They shuffle their decks of cards
(yes, we know they're really leaves) unaware that this is the Titanic

of sorts, for the cat's asleep, its underbelly rotated upwards, its stance
belying the soft-pouched flick knives, the hint of murder. Like the mice,

I'm grateful for the hedge, my gate, my solid brick-and-mortar house.
The wind whistles and I list to starboard. That's what loving you is like.

Next Thursday

I walk around these days with a light in my head.
It's most noticeable at night, shining through my skin
so it looks like elf skin. Once, not quite before moon-down,

I went out to empty my postbox. The light tracked out of my eyes
and pulsed from my nostrils. My veins lit up like a brace of fairy wands.

In the empty post-box I placed the stinging wasp of a kiss.
The postman will deliver it before next Thursday.
When you receive it, I will have turned off the light in my head.

In the dark I am waiting. Moss keeps growing in the dark.
It is soft and inviting. Thursday is a long way off.

In One Breath

The way grass breathes at night,
releasing oxygen in one fell swoop

would make you light-headed
if you could, by some inspired miracle,
shrink in height and, from then on, measure

each seedling's sprout or how a sparrow
comes to light, spangling the blue of the plumbago tree;
a twist and frill of touchpaper flight
which has nothing to do with either you or me.

An Unusual Proposal of Marriage

by a filthy rumpus of dike which glued
together two sides of the same field,

and out of which ricocheted a rat.
It slipstreamed up the shallow bank

and caused a zithering of grass
which parted and closed like a breath

long after the thought it intended
has ended. On the following day we saw it again,

grey body the length of a child's ballet shoe,
death-grin already covered

by a congregation of ants, which, with the sun
on their backs, glittered like crystals.

You turned away, but not before
taking my hand and laying it as an invitation

quite close to your heart which I could feel beating.
And so I knew what you wanted to say

even though the time for saying it was already past
and you were booked to fly out later that afternoon.

Crossing the River

1

A dented coin lay in my path.
I picked it up, wiped off the dirt,
secreted it inside my pocket.
It was summer, the pavement so hot
you could fry an egg on it.
When was that? What day?
The day you upped and left.
I'm ashamed to say I almost forgot.

2

I could imagine you in different rooms,
ceilings studded with chandeliers,
carpets ringed with telescopes.
But not the room in perpetual autumn
with shelves of insects preserved in amber,
their habits freeze-framed, built to last.
You said for the price of a coin
I could have one too. So what did I do?
That night I raided my money-box.

3

My father gave it to me when I was five,
a tickey, silver, very thin,
like a puff of air on a winter's night.
I stuck it on my bedroom ceiling.
From far, it looked like a star.
From near, it looked like a smudge.
It was supposed to keep me in luck
for the rest of my life. In luck or in love.
But I trusted to Fate. It was a mistake.
I threw the tickey away.

4

I lost my money in the river, in
the slithering, slopping uMngeni mud,
quite distant from what I'd imagined as a girl:
coral palaces, couches of mother-of-pearl,
water-babies all sugar-pink and blue,
roads of tourmaline, the road I knew
would bring me back to you.
Without a cent in my pocket
I crossed the river. It was spring.

The Box that I Carry

I carried his heart in a box
and the box was very big,
with a metal flap and bright hinges,
and it weighed a lot in my hands.

And it weighed a lot in my hands
because he had loved so much
and so many things, except me, that is,
and yet I carried his heart in a box

with me wherever I went.
Sometimes I set it on the table
and other times at my feet,
and it weighed a lot in my hands.

I lifted it up to the window to look at it,
then tipped it out on the lawn
for the birds which didn't know why
I'd carried his heart in a box

and that it weighed less than I thought
such a full heart would do. But it
had shrunk to the size of a pea
and I carried his heart in a box

the size of a pill-box, and the box
was very, very tiny, and the edges were
scuffed, and its lock was broken
and out spilled something like pebbles

which weighed a lot in my hands
because this was the weight
of my freedom to close up the box
where once I'd carried his heart.

It is Good

I know my cat for his eyes,
two fur-lined inkwells that break through
any attempt at concentration.
Next comes the soundtrack: sharp mewps
or miniature roller-blades on wood.

What I keep forgetting (and remember,
I'm over 50, now) is patience.
And so I shove him off the bed,
stomp to the doorway and point
in whatever direction he's ordered
to go. Because at this moment
I am God, and it is good.
Then I retreat to my study
(The Realm of All Things)

and try to write, to untether
the black panthers that have been trussed
in the garden shed for years
and let them crack open
the roof of my house, turn
its iron sheeting into bronze,
its rafters to pillars,
its layered insulation to cloth of gold.
Yes, I am God, and it is good.

But, of course, it's no good. The ink stays fast
in the wells. The panthers shrink
to ceramic merchandise. The house could fit
inside the hull of an almond.
My morning stubble is farm-yard thick
and belies the swish of cock's spurs.
My breath is pig-sty potent
and the cat won't come near me.

I coo, croon, smuggle a wad of fish
between my bottom and upper lip
while giving my best Marilyn Monroe pout.
The slothful fur twitches. This is good.
One inkwell opens up, and in it grows
a fish the size of Nineveh and Tarshish put together.
Two leaves unfurl. A flat, pink snake dips
into the bowl of milk as though witch dunking.

Barefoot, I retreat to my study (The Realm
of All Things), press sulphur against phosphorus
to emblazon my cigarette and dispel
all shadow, doubt, recriminations.
It is what it is: a man, a cat, the still-empty page
which, nevertheless, is good.
I inhale with immense satisfaction, watch
the pillar of smoke rising, rising.
Tomorrow, I shall invent Woman.

Bronze Lur[1]

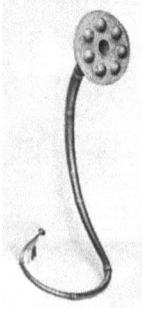

It looks like a highly modernized bathplug,
although that hole in the middle
circled by seven bronze studs
could be quite deceptive.
My wife thinks it looks like
a piece of the sole of a soccer boot.
But I point out it has a tail
like a sting-ray flowing with the current.

She says the bloody thing
could not only fall to pieces,
but the end bit's so small
you'd need very good lungs
to get a sound out of it.

I say the word she's thinking of
is *embouchure,* and I point out, further,
that our neighbour could tell us more
as he was a trombonist.
She says he couldn't have been for long
as he has emphysema.

Looking at it from another angle,
she says it'd be perfect
for our hanging basket,
the one she planted with African violets
and begonias – the ones
I drowned with overwatering.

I reminded her she'd gone away
for three weeks to her mother's
and had left only the barest
of instructions. She replied
I'd also forgotten to mow the lawn.

I should've kept quiet.
Like the lur. After all,
I have no announcements
to make, no reinforcements
to summon. The only ritual
was when the kids left home,
which they did, noisily and untidily.
I notice my wife's still-youthful body
and how it curves most gracefully.
She has such a tiny mouth.

I imagine the lur was made for war.
It summoned the troops, heralded campaigns,
re-aligned territory, frightened the enemy.
My wife does all this, too.

The museum is closed on Mondays.

[1]A long natural blowing horn, without finger holes, that can be straight or curved
in various shapes. Bronze-age lurs were often found in pairs, deposited in bogs
(Denmark, Germany), and consist of a mouthpiece and several pieces and/or pipes.
Opinions differ as to whether they were used in war, or were primarily for ceremonial
or ritual purposes.

Rhino Watch

A cracking sound on the tin roof tonight
makes Buster gather his paws squarely
beneath him, and his belly to leave the couch.
He stands as a pointer-dog would,
body taut as an electric fence.

What does Buster know that's denied to me?
Superior sight, superior hearing, definitely.
Buster's fur loosens back around his bones
as he settles down and begins hunting for fleas.

That arrhythmic cracking sound again:
it sounds like smoky fire
but it would be fire despite the rain,
like the shock of discovering nothing's there,
or that what was there is suddenly gone.

In the morning Buster discovers the carcass
minus horn. His yelping's matched by the sound of flies.
It's the sound we make at the end of breath.
The end of everything. And then —

Lizard

First, it clung to the ceiling, a five-point
changeling shape like swept-up broken glass,
entranced, perhaps, by its inspection
of the history of this house:

how the builders' lines were skew, their angles
laid impure, the airbricks clotted
with plaster residue. The cracks breathe putty,
the parquet, swelled, is insecure.

Without a reason, the creature falls
to the carpet, then crawls from wall to door
like brown foam fleshed
from ocean's floor. Last time

I looked, the lizard's tail was gone,
stopped at the point of life continuing,
which continues on. The creature seeks
another path: this time the mirror,

its flesh now stacked in two. Its ancestry
predates mine, but here we intersect,
warm to cold. At a time when late light slows,
lizard's leathery back is turned to stone.

Inventory of a Cat

Yes, of course you can list them.
Eyes: aquamarines set skew.
Fur: new-formed frost.
Teeth: miniature walrus tusks.

It needn't stop there.
Paw-pads: liquorice and Wicks bubble-gum.
Nose: pink tulle.

This layer-cake of muscle
summits the Roman blind daily,
pushing up into the pelmet
as though breaking into the hereafter.

The inventory
needn't stop there. Let's bring it
fully up to date:
the supple skeleton
wrapped in fish-net veins,
the lowered head like a painted whale
and the frozen radars of her ears.

Last on the list:
the catheter
still lancing her foreleg
with its pygmy arrow.

The part not shown:
her Cupid's dart that pierced
my heart from first to last
and now continues on and on
in boundless flight.

Cardiac Arrest

I found the stone stairs
to the roof, the ones
with a star at the top
if you climb them at evening.

Up, this time not evening
but almost midday, the legs like roots
that will not give way,
the chest with its little alarm-clock
sprung too tight
so that the *snap*

of its works disconnects
the breath from flight.
So down I fell
like Lucifer bathed in fire,
or Persephone on that black road
                    shuffling under.

It was weeks before I came round.
Martha and Tom were there
at my bedside to tell me the story.
I'd been white as marbellite. Then
I'd turned blue. They left
and I cried.

I would like to say I cried
my heart out.
But I suspect I'd left it there
half-way up the stone stair.

For now,
Lucifer's quiet. Persephone
raises her eyes and looks back
at the hospital gates.
It's night. No stars.
The grass is woolly,
the flowers like glass.
My alarm-clock's set, and wound.

The Moon Watch

When you bought me the watch
I could see everything:
the time, the date, the moon
in its different phases.

That was then. Things are different,
now. Oh yes, I can tell the time,
but the date has entered
a myopic cycle of mystery

and the moon itself
is nothing more
than a shrunken-headed sun.
I still have the watch

and I still see everything:
the way time no longer holds you
to me, the single strand of her hair
on your jacket's lapel

like the golden second-hand
brushing across an inscrutable face.
Yes, I see it all.
This watch is unstoppable.

Suitcase

Unburdening myself, I pack away last week's
cloudburst, a plastic sheep, five years of hell
at high school, my first, bumbling kiss,

the grandparents I never met, the scent
of bath oil spilt on the mat, a new-born kitten,
raisin bread, mielie kernels. And, of course,

myself as I will be in my dotage, since
the suitcase can expand to hold it all.
Lastly, I shall leave it at the station

without a label or a ticket, already
at its destination, waiting for the stranger
who will pick it up, treasure it, go on living.

ABOUT THE AUTHOR

Gail Dendy was first published by Nobel Prize winner Harold Pinter and shared a poetry collection with Peabody Winner and Oscar Nominee Norman Corwin. Her collections have appeared, variously, in Britain, South Africa and the United States, and many are held in the National English Literary Museum, Grahamstown; the New Alexandria Library, Egypt; and The Poetry Library, South Bank Centre, London.

Gail has also written plays, short stories, a novel, radio poetry programmes, radio news bulletins, and academic papers and journal articles. Accolades include, inter alia: Winner: SA PEN Millennium Competition (Playwriting); Finalist: Herman Charles Bosman Award (Poetry), South African Science Fiction Society Award (Short Story); Shortlisted: Thomas Pringle Award (Short Story), Sol Plaatje/European Union Poetry Award 2011 and 2012; Longlisted: Plough Poetry Prize (UK). She achieved 'Highly Commended' in the Poetry Space Competition (UK) in 2014 and 2015 and for her unpublished novel/fictionalized memoir in the Dinaane Debut Fiction Award 2014. Long listings include The Twenty in 20 Project (the aim of which was to identify the best South African English-language short stories of the first two decades of democracy), Short Story Day Africa 2014, and the Sol Plaatje/European Poetry Award 2014 and 2017.

Besides words, Gail has a passion for dance. Her early training as a gymnast and ballet dancer morphed into a love of Contemporary Dance. In Johannesburg she trained with Robyn Orlin, whilst overseas she trained at the Bat Dor, Alvin Ailey and London Contemporary Dance theatre studios. In 1991 she was nominated for the inaugural AA Vita Award for Best Performer.

Other books by Gail Dendy

Assault and the Moth. Greville Press Pamphlets, Warwick, UK, 1993. (Editors: Harold Pinter, Anthony Astbury & Geoffrey Godbert)

People Crossing. Snailpress, Cape Town, 1995.

Swimming in the Long Dark Sound. Stride, Gail Dendy; Jennie Fontana & Alyss Thomas, Exeter, UK: 1998.

Painting the Bamboo Tree. Todmorden, UK: Arc, 1999.

The Poetry of Norman Corwin and Gail Dendy. Shirim, Sherman Oaks, Calif: 2002.

The Lady Missionary. Kwela/Snailpress, Cape Town, 2007.

Closer Than That. Dye Hard Press, Johannesburg, 2011.

www.ingramcontent.com/pod-product-compliance
Lightning Source LLC
Chambersburg PA
CBHW010013110426
42741CB00040B/3440